Whole 30 Instant Pot #2019

The Ultimate Whole 30 Instant Pot Cookbook with Easy and Delicious Instant Pot Cooker Recipes

Stewart Brock

Table of contents

Introduction 7

Chapter 1: The Basics of the Whole30 9

What is the Whole30? 9

Some awesome advantages of the Whole30 Diet 9

Guidelines for a mother 10

Some tips for the journey 12

Chapter 2: What to do after the first 30 days? 14

Chapter 3: A look at the Instant Pot 19

What is the Instant Pot? 19

Some amazing Instant Pot benefits 19

The core function buttons of the Instant Pot 21

Steps to cleaning your Instant Pot 22

Chapter 4: Food to Eat and to Avoid 24

Chapter 5: Breakfast 27

Succulent Crispy Potatoes 27

Hearty Eggs Benedict and Cauliflower 28

Generous Early Morning Meat Quiche 30

Delicious Protein "Cakes" 31

Simple Baked Potato 32

Blueberry Flavored Breakfast 33

Beets for The Morning 34

Fine Veggie and Scrambled Eggs 35

All-Time Favorite Egg Devils 36

Chapter 6: Beef, Lamb, and Pork 37

Simple Pork and Saffron Loin 37

Aromatic Bone-In Pork Chops 39

Breath Taking Acorn Pork Chops 41

Mexican Beef in A Pot 43

Awesome Beef Root Chili 45

Divine Goulash 46

The Whole30 Thai Brisket 48

Hearty Kalua Pork Dish 50

The Great Mediterranean Leg Lamb Roast 51

Beef and Potato Casserole Medley 53

Healthy Lamb Rogan Josh 54

Chapter 7: Poultry Recipes 56

Simple Pineapple Chicken 56

Feisty Turmeric Chicken 58

Sweet Potato and Chicken Curry 60

Delightful Harissa Chicken 62

Genius Lime Chicken 64

Creative Lemon Garlic Chicken 65
The Authentic Chicken Tikka Masala 66
Pressure Cooked Crab Legs 67
Everyday Chicken Wings 68
Chapter 8: Seafood Recipes 69
Juicy Salmon and Orange 69
Hearty Salmon Patties 70
Juicy Coconut Fish Curry 71
Authentic Sock Eye Salmon 73
Alternative Fancy Cod Dish 74
Cool Salmon and Broccoli 75
Pineapple and Shrimp Delight 76
Hearty Cooked Lobster 77
Chapter 9: Vegetarian Recipes 78
Gentle Cauliflower Soup 78
Amazing Butter and Garlic Potatoes 80
Healthy Brussels and Pine Nuts 81
Ghee Dredged Baby Carrots 82
Easy Steamed Artichokes 83
Butter and Garlic Green Beans 84
Mashed Cauliflower Meal 85

Healthy Potato Gratin 86
Mixed Summer Vegetable Platter 87
Tasty Carrot and Kale Bowl 88
Indian Spinach and Mustard Dish 89
The All-Natural Sugar-Free Applesauce 91
Rhubarb and Strawberry Compote 92
Chapter 10: Soup and Stew Recipes 93
Exquisite Lobster Bisque 93
Simple Lamb Stew 95
Slightly "Eastern" Lamb Stew 96
The Original Enchilada Soup 98
Very Yummy Chicken Soup 100
Wow-Worthy Creamy Onion Soup 101
Hearty Asparagus Soup 102
Nice Apple Cabbage and Beet Stew 103
Cabbage and Carrot "Hearty Celery" Soup 104
Friendly Butternut Squash Soup 105
Conclusion 106

Introduction

As you may have already guessed from the name, the Whole30 program is a very unique and awesome diet program that encourages you to change your feeding habits for the next 30 days in order to literally "Reset" your body's internal mechanism and make it healthier once again.

The core concept here is that for the next 30 days, you are to get rid of any and all kinds of "Processed" foods from your life and replace them when a good dose of healthy and natural ingredients.

Over the course of 30 days, your body will slowly start to re-adjust itself to the new changes and start repairing your internals and rejuvenate your life source.

All that being said though, we understand that following a strict diet these days is extremely tough, especially due to our busy and hectic schedule.

And that is exactly why I have dedicated this particular book to amazing Whole30 friendly recipes that you can easily whip up using your Instant Pot!

For those of you don't know, the Instant Pot is an absolutely revolutionary kitchen appliance that has the capacity to act as multiple appliances under singlehood.

With an Instant Pot, you won't only be getting a highly modernized electric pressure cooker, but also a steamer, Sauté pan, baking machine, slow cooker and so on!

The Instant Pot is essentially a life-saver for busy individuals and will allow you to have your meals prepared almost 70% faster as compared to more traditional cooking methods!

Since this particular book is dedicated more or less towards beginners, I have dedicated the first chapter of the book, explaining the fundamentals of the Whole30 diet while the next chapters cover the basics of the Instant Pot appliance itself.

Once you are done with the basic, feel free to explore the amazing Whole30 Instant Pot recipes found in this book, that are sure to allow you to encourage you to explore even further and inspire you to follow a healthier lifestyle.

Just be warned, the Whole30 diet requires an extreme level of dedication. If you start your journey, then you have strictly followed the regime for the next consecutive 30 days! If you break down for even a single day, you have to reel back to day 1 and start all over again!

Chapter 1: The Basics of the Whole30

With the intro out of the way, let me start off this booking by giving a brief insight into the diet itself.

Starting off with the most basic question first then:

What is the Whole30?

Developed by Melissa and Dallas Hartwig, the Whole30 diet is an amazing diet that promises an individual to seamlessly improve their psychological and physiological health over a period of 30 days, without sacrifice the foods that they love!

As mentioned in the Intro, the core procedure of the Whole30 diet is to basically "Reset" the whole metabolic system of your body and completely alter how you interact with foods on a daily basis.

If you look at it from a broader perspective, you would notice that the Whole30 diet is actually very much similar to the Paleo diet! However, the Whole30 is actually a bit stricter in terms of imposing a list of allowed ingredients. The outcome is significantly more beneficial too!

At its core, what you have to do is that eliminate various inflammatory food groups such as grains, dairy, legumes, alcohol, sugar etc. in order to allow your body to "Breath" and heal itself slowly.

The restrictions of the diet are should not be looking upon as being a limiting factor to your lifestyle, but rather a means through, which you will be able to re-orient your food habits so that you can enjoy cleaner and simpler foods.

Some awesome advantages of the Whole30 Diet

Now that you have a general idea, let me share some of the health benefits that you will enjoy following the Whole30 diet. Keep in mind, the longer you will follow the diet, the stronger and more profound the benefits will become.

While there are lots of amazing benefits to being experienced, below are some of the core ones:

- The Whole30 diet will largely improve your skin and hair conditions thanks to the abundance of clean and healthy food
- Exposure to clean and healthy food will ensure that your body gets almost 3 times more energy to spend on a daily basis
- Even though the Whole30 diet is not dedicated to losing the weight, the clean and lean lifestyle will actually help to lose weight in the long run. Since you will be abandoning processed food from your diet, your body will eventually start shedding off more pounds that you would expect!
- The elimination of sugar from your diet will actually help you to lower down symptoms of endometriosis and improve your sexual drive and fertility rate
- The balanced intake of the Whole30 will help you to improve your mood and lower down the possibility of suffering from anxiety attacks
- The program will improve your concentration power and help you to stay focused all throughout the day

And believe me when I say this, those are just the tip of the iceberg!

Guidelines for a mother

By now you must be pretty excited to jump into the band-wagon and embark on your Whole30 diet!

However, if you are either a pregnant mother or a breastfeeding lady, there are certain criteria that you should know about before embarking on your quest.

When it comes to pregnancy though, the Whole30 doesn't really need a whole lot of modification; however, it is essential that some minute adjustments are made to the diet.

It should be noted that a high-protein diet such as a Whole30, isn't really that healthy for the growing baby. Generally speaking, pregnant women should have stricter control over protein intake and it should not exceed about 20% of the total consumed calorie.

Key steps that you should keep in mind

- As mentioned earlier, make sure to create a diet plan that is low on protein
- Just in case if you lean more towards a higher protein diet, you should try to eat more fat and carbs to make for missing calories
- After the first 3 months of your pregnancy, try to add an extra 300 calories to your diet in order to make sure that your baby is properly fed
- While usually, Whole30 has a strict policy against snacking, pregnancy will require you to resort to smaller meals throughout the day in order to keep everything in check
- Mercury-containing food such as Tuna, Marlin, Raw Eggs, Swordfish and/or raw meat is to be avoided

Some tips to avoid morning sickness

- Try to keep most or all of your required groceries at home. It will prevent you from needing to go to the shopping market every day and will give you more time to breathe and relax.
- Try to be more flexible when it comes to managing your meal plan. During pregnancy, you will need to alter your meal plan as required.
- Make sure to follow your instinct. If you think that the Whole30 is leaving you exhausted or underfed. Then don't hesitate to take a break and go on a regular diet to keep yourself and the baby packed.

Before taking any supplements, make sure to discuss the diet thoroughly with your dietician.

- Make sure to go for prenatal vitamins to get the appropriate levels of vitamins and minerals
- Try to go for supplementing yourself with about 300mg of DHA per day
- Go for COD Liver Oil as they are an excellent source of Omega -3 fats and Vitamins such as A, D, and K2
- Vitamin D3 plays a great role when it comes to keeping you healthy during pregnancy
- If possible, then go for some healthy homemade bone broth as they are a great source of calcium, magnesium, phosphorus
- Vitamin B Complex will maintain the healthy growth of your baby

- Liver pills are great sources of Vitamins like A, D and E alongside choline and Iron

Alternatively, while you are breastfeeding, you should always keep the following points in mind:

- Make sure to keep your breast empty. Meaning try to feed your baby according to his/her desire and/or empty your breast using a pump after you feed your baby. An empty breast will result in faster milk generation.
- While breastfeeding, make sure to keep your daily calories intake above 1800, otherwise, it might result in less milk production.
- Keep your daily carb above 100g
- Make sure to keep drinking as much water as you can
- Just like pregnancy, you should try to take small sized meals throughout the day. Make sure to include a good amount of protein, fat, and carbs in your diet as well. The limitation of protein is only needed during pregnancy.

Supplements to consider while breastfeeding

- Go for COD Liver Oil as they are an excellent source of Omega -3 fats and Vitamins such as A, D, and K2
- Vitamin D3 plays a great role when it comes to keeping you healthy during pregnancy
- If possible, then go for some healthy homemade bone broth as they are a great source of calcium, magnesium, phosphorus

Some tips for the journey

And to top it off, the following tips should help you to further enhance your experience with the Whole30 program and ensure that you are able to reap its full potential.

- Make sure that you have fully set up your mind and have committed yourself to the journey
- Instead of planning for the 30 days, you should plan out the first 2 weeks first. Breaking down the whole journey will make it easier for you.
- Clear out the house off any foods that are not-Whole30 compliant
- Plan the meals beforehand

- Mix and match the schedule to create your very own perfect plan! You can also take help from the meal plan provided in this book as well.
- Make sure to set one day aside to prepare your meals ahead of time.
- Try to keep food-related socializing events at a minimum
- The Whole30 community is full of inspiring stories and figures. If you ever start feeling left out, just browse the web and you will get a plethora of support materials.
- Try to keep yourself distracted from food cravings.
- And most importantly, never give up

Chapter 2: What to do after the first 30 days?

It almost always seems that this is the point where people find themselves confused the most and are unable to decide "What do to after the first 30 days?"

Well, this is where this particular section comes in. Here, I will try to briefly share what you should do once you are done with your initial 30 days of the Whole30 program.

Now, before I start going into details, you should learn to appreciate the fact that the first 30 days of the Whole30 challenge, aren't necessarily the end of the program itself.

Rather, you should look at them as being a means to a new end, or a means to another chapter of your life.

Take some time to grasp that idea and anchor it in your head. Good?

Let's move on now.

So, once you are done with the first 30 days of the diet, there are actually 3 more steps that you should be aware of.

I will try to briefly break each of them down for your pleasure.

Step 1: Reintroduction

So, once you are done with the first step of your program, which is the 30 days challenge, the next step that you should consider is the "Reintroduction" phase.

This phase is somewhat like a science experiment, where you try to introduce some of the food groups that you had eliminated, and assess their impact on your body.

If you find that your body is reacting positively to them, you get to keep it for the remaining days.

However, if you see that your body is not reacting properly, then you should eliminate it for good.

A sample sequence to follow might look like:

Day 1: You may start off by trying to re-introduced legumes and evaluate how they work.

Day 4: After a 3 days trial run, select the legumes that you want to keep and move on to re-introducing Non-Gluten grains such as corn tortilla chips or white rice.

Day 7: This should be followed by an evaluation of Dairy products. Some cheese or ice creams are to be considered during this phase.

Day 10: Finally, you should evaluate Gluten -Containing Grains to see how they react to your body.

It should be noted that throughout all of these processes, you are to stick to your usual Whole30 diet while only including the experimental food group that is being assessed.

Step 2: Sharing Your Knowledge and Experience

Since the conception, the Whole30 program, followers all around the world have banded together and formed a huge community of thinkers, helpers, and enthusiasts.

Throughout various get-together and meetings, these hearty individuals try to share their success stories of how Whole30 helped them in order to inspire and encourage others to follow along with their footsteps.

Once you have completed the first 30 days, we also recommend that you share your personal success story to the world and help them understand what this diet is all about.

If you feel uncomfortable attending meetings, then you can always go for various blogs and online groups.

While writing or telling your story, some points that you might want to include might be:

- How you brought control over your food eating habits
- How Whole30 helped to eliminate various symptoms or conditions
- How the biomarkers such as triglycerides, blood pressure or blood sugar level improved
- How a Whole30 diet helped you to trim down your weight and gain back your confidence
- How it helped to become pregnant
- How Whole30 helped you to be at Peace with yourself
- How you were able to transfer the Whole30 habits to other aspects of your life and so on...

Step 3: The Journey Up Front

Once you are done with your 30 days, it is highly recommended that you try to keep following the Whole30 program for as long as possible as it will help you to stay healthier for longer.

However, we understand that it is not always possible to follow the program properly as humanly temptations get the best of you.

So, to keep yourself in check during those moments, you should try to keep the following steps in mind:

- Keep focusing on your Whole30 based meals everything single day as long as you can without breaks or any kind of "Cheat Day". Should the lust for sugar come creeping back to you, go for something very minute, just enough to control the temptation. But don't give into it!
- However, should you stumble upon something that is just too irresistible or perhaps something that is culturally or religiously important to you, make a small exception and assess if the food is actually worth it? If it helps, then you can follow the below given that will greatly help you assess the food and decide if eating it would be a good idea.

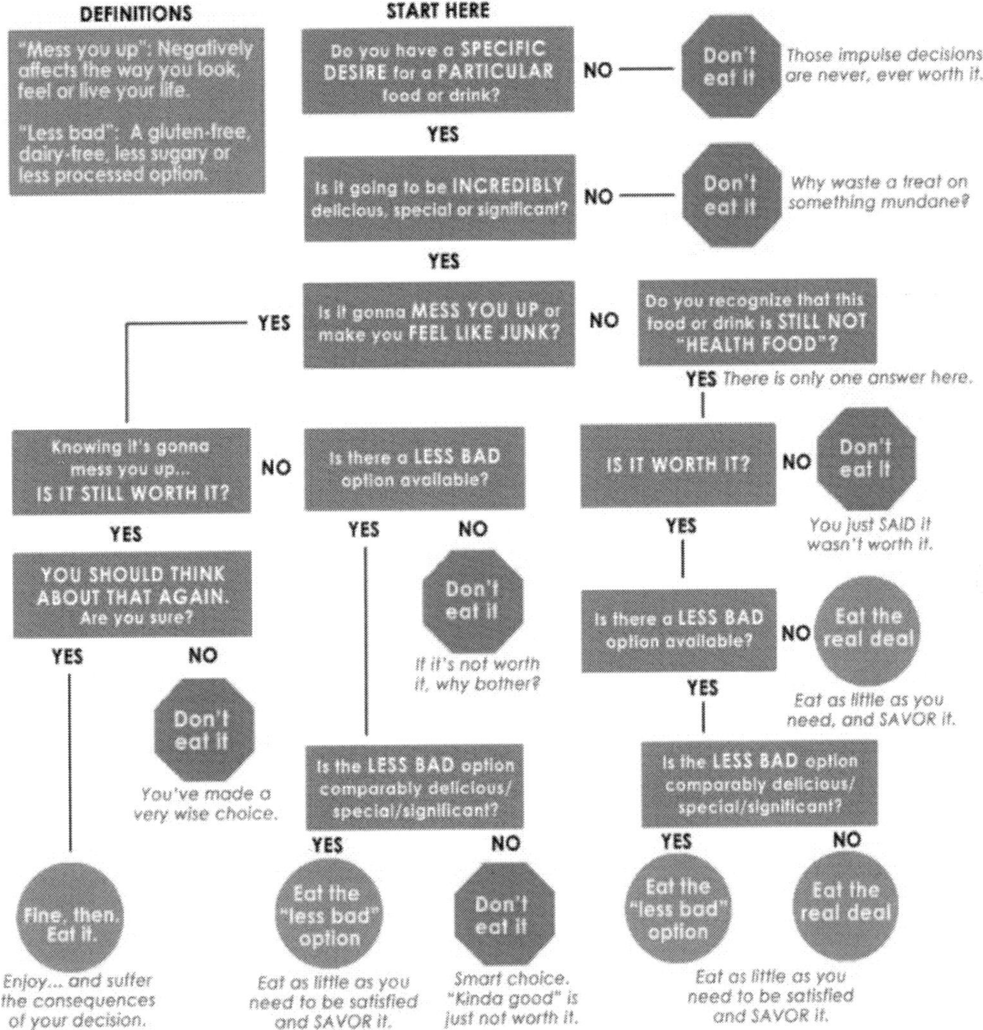

- Assuming that you have decided to let yourself go, make sure to take your time while eating the meal. Eat is conscious, trying to maintain your diet as much as you can. A good way to do this is to eat just as little as you need until you are able to control your temptation. Once you are ready, keep the remaining for later use.

- Once you are done with your meal, make sure to not feel guilt or shame! What is done is done right? There's no turning back. So, it's better to just accept the fact that you have made a conscious decision and give yourself some slack. Try to keep yourself together and keep moving forward, trying to follow your Whole30 properly.

Chapter 3: A look at the Instant Pot

Now that the basics of the Whole30 are covered, let me share a little bit about the Instant Pot itself.

What is the Instant Pot?

To keep things short and simple, the Instant Pot is at its core, one of the most advanced Electric Pressure cooker that comes packed with a wide variety of features that makes it one of the most versatile multi-cookers to date.

Using the single pot cooker, you will essentially be able to steam, bake, Sauté, warm and even slow cook to prepare different types of meals in an instant!

Some amazing Instant Pot benefits

The list of benefits that you will use an Instant Pot will make up a huge list! Therefore, to keep things short and simple, below are some of the crucial ones that you should know about!

One Pot that does it all

The Instant Pot is designed to be extremely versatile and flexible to use. This single appliance has the capacity to be used as multiple cooking appliances, which not only saves your money but also your time as well! This is pretty much the "One Pot to Rule Them All"

Defrost-Be Gone

The Instant Pot is one of that rare appliances that actually allows you to directly cook frozen meals, saving a lot of time. The pressure method can easily defrost and tenderize frozen meat.

Easy cooking and cleaning

Let me start off with the most obvious one first! The Instant Pot will allow you to cook everything in just a single pot, which essentially means that you will be able to do all of your cooking without making a huge mess in the kitchen. The flawless sealing mechanism of the Instant Pot further helps to keep any kind of odor or debris locked inside the pot and the stainless-steel construction makes it very easy to clean.

Built to last

Since the Instant Pot is basically made Stainless Steel, this is an appliance that is made to last! And as an added bonus, the Stainless-Steel construction does not hamper with the flavors of the meal as well, so you can rest easy knowing that the flavors of your meal are preserved to perfection.

Chemical free Coating

Every single Instant Pot appliance is made following extremely high health standards. Therefore, no chemical coating is used in the interior part of the pot that helps the appliance to stay completely free from harmful chemicals that might otherwise hamper the flavor of your meal and negatively impact your health.

Delayed cooking mechanism

The delayed free cooking mechanism allows food to stay warm and moist as long as they are in the pot. This allows you to serve hot and delicious food, anytime you want, straight out of the pot!

Restaurant Quality Dish at Home

Yes, you read that right! Following the recipes found in this book and using the various functionalities of the Instant Pot, you will actually be able to create premium restaurant quality dishes right at home!

Saves space in Kitchen

The versatility of the Instant Pot and its capacity act as multiple appliances allow you to get rid of the steamer, Sauté pan, slow cooker, pressure cooker and a myriad of different appliances and use the Ninja Foodi for everything.

High-Pressure kills microbes

The excellent way in which the Instant Pot cook, ensure that the temperature inside is able to reach sufficiently high enough levels during pressure cooking to ensure that 99% of harmful microbes are killed during the process. In fact, the Instant Pot is even able to kill significantly more resistant microbes as well.

The core function buttons of the Instant Pot

Some people often think that using the Instant Pot might be rather difficult, which is understandable as the plethora of options here might seem a little bit jarring to absolute newcomers.

However, if you know what each button does, then you should not have any problem using the Instant Pot!

To keep things simple. I have briefly tried to explain all the basic functionalities of the core Instant Pot buttons below.

Sauté: You should go for this button if you want to sauté your vegetables or produces inside your inner pot while keeping the lid open. It is possible to adjust the level of brownness you desire by pressing the modify button as well. As a small tip here, you can very quickly push the Sauté Button followed by the Adjust Button two times to simmer your food.

Keep Warm/Cancel: Using this button, you will be able to turn your pressure cooker off. Alternatively, you can use the adjust button to keep maintaining a warm temperature ranging from 293 degrees F (on average) to 332-degree F (at more) degree Celsius depending on what you need.

Manual: This is pretty much an all-rounder button which gives a higher level of flexibility to the user. Using this button followed by the + or – buttons, you will be able to set the exact duration of cooking time which you require.

Soup: This mode will set the cooker to a high-pressure mode giving 30 minutes of cooking time (at normal); 40 minutes (at more); 20 minutes (at less)

Meat/Stew: This mode will set the cooker to a high-pressure mode giving 35 minutes of cooking time (at normal); 45 minutes (at more); 20 minutes (at less)

Bean/Chili: This mode will set the cooker to a high-pressure mode giving 30 minutes of cooking time (at normal); 40 minutes (at more); 25 minutes (at less)

Poultry: This mode will set the cooker to a high-pressure mode giving 15 minutes of cooking time (at normal); 30 minutes (at more); 5 minutes (at less)

Rice: This is a fully automated mode which cooks rice on low pressure. It will adjust the timer all by itself depending on the amount of water/rice present in the inner cooking pot.

Multi-Grain: This mode will set the cooker to a high-pressure mode giving 40 minutes of cooking time (at normal); 45 minutes (at more); 20 minutes (at less)

Porridge: This mode will set the cooker to a high-pressure mode giving 20 minutes of cooking time (at normal); 30 minutes (at more); 15 minutes (at less)

Steam: This will set your pressure cooker to high pressure with 10 minutes of cooking time at normal. 15 minutes cook time at more and 3 minutes cook time at less. Keep in mind that it is advised to use this mode with a steamer basket or rack for best results.

Slow Cooker: This button will normally set the cooker at 4-hour mode. However, you change the temperature by keeping it at 190-201-degree Fahrenheit (at low); 194-205-degree Fahrenheit (at normal); 199-210-degree Fahrenheit (at high);

Pressure: This button allows you to alter between high and low-pressure settings.

Yogurt: This setting should be used when you are in the mood for making yogurt in individual pots or jars

Timer: This button will allow you to either decrease or increase the time by using the timer button and pressing the + or – buttons.

Steps to cleaning your Instant Pot

Using your Instant Pot over time is bound to accumulate lots of dirt and debris. Keeping it clean is the secret to increasing the longevity of your appliance!

The following steps should help you easily keep your Instant Pot in tip-top condition.

The Base and Heating element: The base of the Instant Pot is where you will find the microprocessor and heating element, so you should be cautious while cleaning this part. The key is to ensure that you don't put it in the dishwasher! Rather, use a simple damp cloth and wipe the outside of the housing. The inside of the housing can also be cleaned using a slightly wet cloth, just make sure to dry the whole appliance before using it again.

Stainless Steel Inner Pot and Rack: The inner pot of your Instant Pot is carefully designed using food grade 304 stainless steel, that ensure that no chemical coating is used here. Despite being extremely durable, it is still possible for the inner pot to show some form of discoloration! To deal with this, simply use a non-abrasive stainless-steel cleaner and wipe it gently. If you want to take things further, just soak the inner pot under vinegar for 5 minutes and rinse it gently under water to remove the marks.

The Lid: Lucky for you, the lid is actually completely dished washer safe! If you want to wash it, simply remove it and put it in your dishwasher. However, before doing so, make sure to remove the sealing ring and anti-block shield before putting it to the washer.

Anti-Block Shield and Sealing Ring: The Anti-Block Shield and Sealing Ring are both made of very high-quality heat-resistant materials and can be washed with warm, soapy water. Make sure to dry them before putting them back into place.

Condensation Collector: This is the chamber that collects all the condensed liquid and you should clean it from time to time. The process is very straight forward here, just simply removing it and wash it under cold water.

Chapter 4: Food to Eat and to Avoid

While you are following the Whole30 program, it is essential that you maintain your food intake and get rid of certain ingredients to reap maximum benefits.

To help you understand the requirements, the following list should help you understand the food list of a Whole30 program.

- Almond flour
- Almond milk
- Arrowroot Powder
- Bacon
- Bean Sprouts
- Cacao
- Canola Oil
- Olive Oil
- Carob
- Chia
- Citric Acid
- Coconut Flour
- Coconut Water
- Coffee
- Dates
- Flax Seed
- Fruit Juice
- Guar Gum
- Green Beans
- Hemp Seeds
- Larabars
- Mayonnaise (Homemade)
- Mustard
- Nutritional Yeast
- Potatoes (Added in August 2014)
- Salt

- Sunflower Oil
- Snow Peas
- Tahini
- Water Kefir
- Egg

To elaborate, the following food groups are completely allowed:

- Vegetables
- Fruits
- Unprocessed ed Meat
- Seafood
- Nuts and Seeds
- Oils and Ghee

Alternatively, these are the ones that you should steer clear from during the 30 days.

- Amino Acids
- Buckwheat
- Carob
- Deep Fried Chips
- Dark Chocolate
- Chewing Gum
- Hummus
- Paleo Bread
- Paleo Ice Cream
- Pancakes
- Any kind of Protein Shakes
- Quinoa
- Stevia Leaf
- Vanilla Extract

To elaborate, the food groups to avoid are:

- Dairy products such as cow milk, cream, yogurt, kefir, butter etc. (only clarified butter/ghee is allowed)

- Any kind of grains such as corn, wheat, quinoa, millet etc.
- Alcoholic Beverages
- Legumes such as peas, lentils, peanuts or even soy such as tofu, miso or Edamame

Chapter 5: Breakfast

Succulent Crispy Potatoes

Serving: 4

Prep Time: 5 minutes

Cook Time: 5-10 minutes

Ingredients

- 1 cup of water
- pound potatoes, sliced into cubes
- 2 tablespoons ghee
- Salt and pepper to taste
- ¼ cup chives, chopped

Directions

1. Add water to your Instant Pot
2. Add potatoes and lock lid, cook on HIGH pressure for 5 minutes
3. Release pressure naturally
4. Set your pot to Sauté mode and add ghee, let it heat up
5. Add boiled potatoes
6. Season with salt and pepper and cook until crispy
7. Toss with chives and serve
8. Enjoy!

Nutrition Values (Per Serving)

- Calories: 135
- Fat: 6g
- Carbohydrates: 18g
- Protein: 2g

Hearty Eggs Benedict and Cauliflower

Serving: 2

Prep Time: 5 minutes

Cook Time: 5-10 minutes

Ingredients

- Whole30 friendly cooking spray
- 1 cup cauliflower, sliced
- 1 cup of water
- 2 whole eggs
- 2 teaspoons lemon juice
- 1 egg yolk
- Salt and pepper to taste
- 1 tablespoon ghee

Directions

1. Take your egg cup molds and spray them with oil
2. Add cauliflower to Instant Pot
3. Add water and place steamer rack inside the pot, put molds on top of the rack
4. Crack eggs into the bowl and transfer each bowl into the molds (without breaking the yolk)
5. Lock lid and cook on HIGH pressure for 2 minutes
6. Quick release pressure
7. Drain cauliflower and take out egg cups
8. Add lemon juice, egg yolks, salt and pepper to your blender, the process for 30 seconds
9. Pour over cauliflower and serve
10. Enjoy!

Nutrition Values (Per Serving)

- Calories: 160

- Fat: 13g
- Carbohydrates: 4g
- Protein: 8g

Generous Early Morning Meat Quiche

Serving: 4

Prep Time: 5 minutes

Cook Time: 30-35 minutes

Ingredients

- 1 cup of water
- 6 whole eggs, beaten
- ½ cup almond milk
- Salt and pepper to taste
- 1 cup ground beef, cooked
- 1 slice ham, diced
- 2 green onions, chopped

Directions

1. Place steamer rack in your Pot
2. Add water
3. Take a bowl and beat in eggs, milk, season with salt and pepper
4. Place ground beef, ham and green onion in small baking dish
5. Pour egg mix on top and cover with foil
6. Transfer baking dish on top of rack and lock lid
7. Cook on HIGH pressure for 30 minutes
8. Quick release pressure
9. Serve and enjoy!

Nutrition Values (Per Serving)

- Calories: 370
- Fat: 14g
- Carbohydrates: 3g
- Protein: 10g

Delicious Protein "Cakes"

Serving: 4

Prep Time: 5 minutes

Cook Time: 5 minutes

Ingredients

- 6 whole eggs, beaten
- 1 cup bacon, shredded
- 1 cup baby spinach
- 1 cup tomatoes, chopped

Directions

1. Take a bowl and add beaten eggs, stir in cream cheese
2. Add bacon, spinach, mozzarella cheese, and tomatoes and mix well until a nice batter form
3. Pour the batter into your muffin cups
4. Add 1 cup of water to your pot
5. Wrap the muffin tins with foil and transfer them to the pot
6. Allow them to cook on HIGH pressure for 5 minutes
7. Release the pressure naturally and serve
8. Enjoy!

Nutrition Values (Per Serving)

- Calories: 268
- Fat: 10g
- Carbohydrates: 41g
- Protein: 5g

Simple Baked Potato

Serving: 4

Prep Time: 5 minutes

Cook Time: 30-40 minutes

Ingredients

- 1 cup of water
- 2 pounds medium baking potatoes, washed and scrubbed

Directions

1. Wash the potatoes carefully and add them to your pot
2. Make sure to pierce the sides of the potatoes thoroughly using a fork
3. Add a cup of water
4. Pre-heat your oven to 450 degrees Fahrenheit
5. Lock up the lid and cook the potatoes for 10 minutes over HIGH pressure
6. Allow the pressure to release naturally over 10 minutes
7. Take tongs and take the small potatoes out and transfer them to the middle rack of your oven, bake for 10-15 minutes (turn the heat off)
8. Repeat with the large potatoes for 10 minutes (do not turn the heat on again)
9. Enjoy!

Nutrition Values (Per Serving)

- Calories: 150
- Fat: 0g
- Carbohydrates: 39g
- Protein: 6g

Blueberry Flavored Breakfast

Serving: 2

Prep Time: 5 minutes

Cook Time: 30-35 minutes

Ingredients

- 1 and ½ cups of water
- ½ cup almond milk
- ¼ cup vegan yogurt
- ¼ cup blueberries, sliced
- Few drops of vanilla extract
- Pinch of cinnamon powder
- 1 tablespoon chia seeds

Directions

1. Add water to your Instant Pot
2. Take a mason jar and add all the listed ingredients, cover the jar with foil
3. Transfer pot to your Instant pot and lock lid, cook on HIGH pressure for 3 minutes
4. Release pressure naturally over 10 minutes
5. Serve and enjoy!

Nutrition Values (Per Serving)

- Calories: 339
- Fat: 31g
- Carbohydrates: 16g
- Protein: 4g

Beets for The Morning

Serving: 4

Prep Time: 10 minutes +30 minutes

Cook Time: 1 minute

Ingredients

- 6 medium beets
- 1 cup of water
- Salt and pepper to taste
- Splash of balsamic vinegar
- Extra virgin olive for drizzle

Directions

1. Wash the beets well and trim them to ½ inch long portions
2. Add 1 cup of water to your pot
3. Place a steamer insert on top of the pot and arrange the beets on top
4. Lock up the lid and cook on HIGH pressure for 1 minute
5. Release the pressure naturally
6. Open up the lid and allow the beets to cool
7. Slice the top of the skin carefully
8. Slice the beets in uniform portions and season with a bit of pepper and salt
9. Add just a splash of balsamic vinegar and marinate for 30 minutes
10. Add extra olive oil and serve!

Nutrition Values (Per Serving)

- Calories: 166
- Fats: 0.4g
- Carbs:15g
- Fiber:3g

Fine Veggie and Scrambled Eggs

Serving: 2

Prep Time: 5 minutes

Cook Time: 30-35 minutes

Ingredients

- 4 eggs, beaten
- 1 tablespoon almond milk
- Salt and pepper to taste
- 1 tablespoon olive oil
- 1 onion, diced
- ¼ cup tomato, chopped

Directions

1. Take a bowl and beat in eggs, milk, salt, and pepper
2. Set your pot to Sauté mode and add oil, let it heat up
3. Add onion and tomato, Sauté for until soft
4. Add egg mixture and cook until nice and coked
5. Garnish with a little bit of chopped green onion if you prefer
6. Enjoy!

Nutrition Values (Per Serving)

- Calories: 229
- Fat: 17g
- Carbohydrates: 8g
- Protein: 12g

All-Time Favorite Egg Devils

Serving: 6

Prep Time: 5 minutes

Cook Time: 6 minutes

Ingredients

- 8 large eggs
- 1 cup of water
- Guacamole as needed
- Sliced radishes as needed
- Whole30 mayonnaise as needed
- Furikake as needed

Directions

1. Add water to your Instant Pot
2. Place steamer rack inside the pot, arrange eggs on the rack
3. Lock lid and cook on HIGH pressure for 6 minutes
4. Release pressure naturally and transfer eggs to the iced water bowl
5. Peel after 5 minutes
6. Cut them in half
7. Garnish with dressings of Guacamole, sliced radishes, and mayonnaise
8. Enjoy!

Nutrition Values (Per Serving)

- Calories: 70
- Fat: 6g
- Carbohydrates: 1g
- Protein: 3g

Chapter 6: Beef, Lamb, and Pork

Simple Pork and Saffron Loin

Serving: 4

Prep Time: 5 minutes

Cook Time: 10-15 minutes

Ingredients

- 12 dried Mexican Red Chilies
- 3 tablespoons fresh thyme leaves
- 2 tablespoons packed oregano leaves, chopped
- 2 tablespoons smoked paprika
- 1 tablespoon garlic, minced
- ½ teaspoon salt
- ½ teaspoon saffron threads
- 3 tablespoons olive oil
- 2 medium green bell pepper, stemmed and cored, chopped
- 1 piece 2 and ½ pounds boneless pork loin, cut into ½ inch pieces

Directions

1. De-stem and de-seed your chilies and tear into small portions
2. Transfer them to a medium sized bowl and add boiling water, allow them to soak for 20 minutes
3. Drain the chilies into a colander and set them in the sink
4. Transfer to a blender and add oregano, thyme, salt, smoked paprika, saffron and garlic
5. Cover and blend until smooth
6. Cover it and blend
7. Set your pot to Sauté mode and add bell peppers, cook for 3 minutes
8. Add pork and stir for 6 minutes
9. Lock up the lid and cook for 10 minutes at high pressure

10. Quickly release the pressure of your pot
11. Unlock and serve

Nutrition Values (Per Serving)

- Calories: 872
- Fat: 68g
- Carbohydrates: 54g
- Protein: 86g

Aromatic Bone-In Pork Chops

Serving: 4

Prep Time: 4-5 hours

Cook Time: 20 minutes

Ingredients

- 4 and ¾ of thick bone-in pork chops
- Salt and pepper to taste
- ¼ cup divided clarified butter
- 1 cup baby carrots
- 1 onion, chopped
- 1 cup vegetables
- 3 tablespoons Worcestershire sauce

Directions

1. Take a bowl and add pork chops, season with salt and pepper
2. Take a skillet and place it over medium heat
3. Add 2 teaspoon of butter and heat up
4. Add pork chops and brown them for 3-5 minutes per side
5. Transfer to a plate
6. Add 2 tablespoon of butter to your Instant Pot
7. Set the pot to Sauté mode
8. Add carrots and onion and Sauté them for a few minutes
9. Pour broth and Worcestershire sauce
10. Add pork chops and lock up the lid
11. Cook on HIGH pressure for 13 minutes
12. Release the pressure naturally over 10 minutes
13. Enjoy and serve!

Nutrition Values (Per Serving)

- Calories: 715

- Fat: 37.4g
- Carbohydrates: 2g
- Protein: 20.7g

Breath Taking Acorn Pork Chops

Serving: 4

Prep Time: 10 minutes

Cook Time: 10 minutes

Ingredients

- 2 tablespoons clarified butter
- 4 and ½ inch thick bone-in pork loin
- ½ teaspoon salt
- 2 medium acorn squash, peeled and deseeded, cut into eighths
- 3 tablespoons dried sage
- ½ teaspoon dried thyme
- ½ teaspoon ground cinnamon
- ¾ cup chicken broth

Directions

1. The first step here is to set your pot to sauté mode and melt in 1 tablespoon of butter
2. Season your chops with pepper and salt and toss them in your pot and cook for 4 minutes
3. Transfer the chops to a plate and repeat to cook and brown the rest
4. Then, add in the chops in a single layer and toss in the squash, sprinkle some thyme, sage, and cinnamon all over
5. Pour in the broth
6. Lock up the lid and let it cook for about 10 minutes at high pressure
7. Quick release the pressure and transfer the chops to a plate
8. Mound the squash around them nicely and ladle up the sauce (if any) all over the chops

Nutrition Values (Per Serving)

- Calories: 348

- Fat: 18g
- Carbohydrates: 2g
- Protein: 42g

Mexican Beef in A Pot

Serving: 4

Prep Time: 10 minutes

Cook Time: 35 minutes

Ingredients

- 2 and ½ pounds boneless beef short ribs
- 1 tablespoon chili powder
- 1 and ½ teaspoons salt
- 1 tablespoon clarified butter
- 1 medium onion, thinly sliced
- 1 tablespoon tomato sauce
- 6 garlic cloves, peeled and smashed
- ½ cup roasted tomato salsa
- ½ cup bone broth
- ½ teaspoon red boat fish sauce
- Fresh ground black pepper
- ½ cup cilantro, minced
- 2 radishes, thinly sliced

Directions

1. Take a large sized bowl and add cubed beef, chili powder, salt and stir
2. Set your pot to Sauté mode and add fat, allow it to melt
3. Add garlic, tomato paste and Sauté for 30 seconds
4. Add seasoned beef, fish sauce, salsa and stock
5. Lock up the lid and cook on MEAT/STEW for 35 minutes
6. Release the pressure naturally over 10 minutes
7. Season with pepper and salt
8. Enjoy!

Nutrition Values (Per Serving)

- Calories: 308
- Fats: 18g
- Carbs:21g
- Fiber:2g

Awesome Beef Root Chili

Serving: 4

Prep Time: 5 minutes

Cook Time: 30 minutes

Ingredients

- 10 ounces beets, sliced
- 1 cup ground beef, cooked
- 1 and 1/3 cup carrots, diced
- 1 and 1/3 cup sweet potato, peeled and diced
- 10- and 2/3-ounces pumpkin
- 1 teaspoon salt
- 2 teaspoons dried basil
- 2/3 teaspoon cinnamon
- 13 and 1/3 beef bone broth
- 3 cups beef bone broth
- 1 and 1/3 tablespoons apple cider vinegar

Directions

1. Add beets to a food processor and puree until smooth
2. Transfer the beets to the pot with remaining ingredients
3. Lock up the lid and cook on HIGH pressure for 10 minutes
4. Release naturally and enjoy!

Nutrition Values (Per Serving)

- Calories: 271
- Fat: 20g
- Carbohydrates: 5g
- Protein: 13g

Divine Goulash

Serving: 4

Prep Time: 5 minutes

Cook Time: 15 minutes

Ingredients

- 1-2 pounds extra-lean ground beef
- 2 teaspoons olive oil + extra 11 teaspoons
- 1 large red bell pepper, stemmed and seeded
- 1 large onion, cut into short strips
- 1 tablespoon garlic, minced
- 2 tablespoons sweet paprika
- ½ teaspoon hot paprika
- 4 cups beef stock
- 2 cans (14 ounces each), tomatoes, diced

Directions

1. Set your pot to Sauté mode and add 2 tablespoons of olive oil
2. Add ground beef to the pot and keep cooking and stirring until it breaks
3. Once the beef is browned up, transfer it to another bowl
4. Cut up the stem off the pepper and deseed them
5. Cut them up into strips
6. Cut the onions into short strips
7. Add a teaspoon of olive oil to the pot and add onion and pepper
8. Add minced garlic, hot paprika, sweet paprika, and cook for 2-3 minutes
9. Add beef stock and tomatoes
10. Add ground beef and lock up the lid
11. Cook on LOW pressure for 15 minutes on SOUP mode
12. Quick release and enjoy!

Nutrition Values (Per Serving)

- Calories: 283
- Fat: 13g
- Carbohydrates: 13g
- Protein: 30g

The Whole30 Thai Brisket

Serving: 4

Prep Time: 5 minutes

Cook Time: 35-40 minutes

Ingredients

- 3 pounds of grass-fed beef brisket, cubed
- 2 teaspoons salt
- 1 tablespoon Thai curry paste
- 1 and ½ cups full fat coconut milk, extra ½ cup as well
- 2 tablespoons coconut amino
- 2 tablespoons apple juice
- 1 tablespoon Red Boat Fish Sauce
- 2 small onion, chopped
- 2 large carrots, peeled and chopped
- A handful of cilantro and scallions

Directions

1. Take a large sized bowl and add the cubed-up beef
2. Season them with salt
3. Add curry paste and give it a nice stir
4. Pour coconut milk, apple juice, coconut amino, fish sauce and stir well
5. Add onion, potatoes, beef cubes and carrots and give it a nice stir
6. Lock up the lid and set your pot to MEAT mode
7. Cook for 35 minutes
8. Release the pressure naturally and transfer the meat to a serving platter
9. Pour the veggies and sauce to a blender alongside ½ a cup of coconut milk
10. Puree and pour the sauce over the beef
11. Enjoy!

Nutrition Values (Per Serving)

- Calories: 362
- Fat: 24g
- Carbohydrates: 27g
- Protein: 14g

Hearty Kalua Pork Dish

Serving: 4

Prep Time: 5 minutes

Cook Time: 35-40 minutes

Ingredients

- 1 whole (4-5 pounds) pork shoulder
- 1 tablespoon bacon fat
- 1 teaspoon salt
- ½ cup pineapple, diced
- 1 teaspoon fish sauce
- 1 tablespoon liquid smoke
- ½ cup of water

Directions

1. Set your pot to Sauté mode
2. Cut up the pork into two individual pieces and add the bacon fat to the pot
3. Add the shoulders and sear it for about 2-3 minutes on each side to brown them
4. Sprinkle a bit of salt on top of your pork
5. Add fish sauce, pineapple, liquid smoke and water to the pot
6. Lock up the lid and cook it over 90 minutes (over manual mode)
7. After 90 minutes, allow the pressure to release naturally over 10 minutes
8. Remove the pork from the pot and pour the juices into a jar
9. Take two forks and shred the pork
10. Add the juice to the pork and serve!

Nutrition Values (Per Serving)

- Calories: 357
- Fat: 28g
- Carbohydrates: 0g
- Protein: 25g

The Great Mediterranean Leg Lamb Roast

Serving: 4

Prep Time: 5 minutes

Cook Time: 50 minutes

Ingredients

- 2 tablespoons olive oil
- 5-6 pounds lamb leg, boneless
- 1 teaspoon salt
- 1 bay leaf, crushed
- ½ teaspoon pepper
- 1 teaspoon marjoram
- 1 teaspoon sage
- 3 garlic cloves, minced
- 1 teaspoon ginger
- 1 teaspoon thyme
- 2 cups broth
- 2 and ½ pounds potatoes, peeled and cut into 2-3-inch pieces
- 2-3 tablespoons arrowroot powder + 1/3 cup water

Directions

1. Set your pot to Sauté mode and add olive oil
2. Add the roast and swirl it around to ensure that it is coated with the oil
3. Sear on one side and flip over, sear the other side
4. Sprinkle salt, pepper, and herbs
5. Add broth
6. Lock up the lid and cook on HIGH pressure for 50 minutes
7. Release the pressure quickly
8. Check if the potatoes are cooked well
9. Take a slotted spoon and transfer the potatoes alongside the roast to a serving platter

10. Cover and keep them warm
11. Whisk in the prepared arrowroot mixture into the pot and wait until thick (keep the pot in Sauté mode during this step)
12. Pour the sauce over the roast and enjoy!

Nutrition Values (Per Serving)

- Calories: 487
- Fat: 45g
- Carbohydrates: 0g
- Protein: 19g

Beef and Potato Casserole Medley

Serving: 4

Prep Time: 5 minutes

Cook Time: 5-10 minutes

Ingredients

- 1-pound ground beef
- 2 cups potatoes, cubed
- 2 cups beef broth
- 2 cups tomato sauce
- 2 tablespoons clarified butter
- 1 yellow onion, chopped
- 5 broccoli florets
- 1 cup whole30 friendly mayonnaise

Directions

1. Set your pot to Sauté mode and add butter, allow the butter to melt
2. Add onion and caramelize it for a few minutes
3. Add beef and lock up the lid
4. Cook on HIGH pressure for 5 minutes
5. Release the pressure naturally and give it a nice stir
6. Add potatoes, broccoli and beef broth
7. Lock up the lid and cook on LOW pressure for 5 minutes
8. Release the pressure naturally and stir n spices and tomato sauce
9. Top it up with mayo and enjoy!

Nutrition Values (Per Serving)

- Calories: 144
- Fat: 7g
- Carbohydrates: 2g
- Protein: 18g

Healthy Lamb Rogan Josh

Serving: 4

Prep Time: 5 minutes

Cook Time: 50 minutes

Ingredients

- 1-pound lamb, deboned and cut into 1 and ½ inch cubes
- 4 tablespoons coconut cream
- ½ teaspoon Garam masala

For Spices

- 1 tablespoon olive oil
- 2 bay leaves
- 3 cardamom pods, cracked
- 2 whole cloves
- 1 and ½ teaspoons cumin seeds
- 1 and ½ teaspoon fennel seeds
- 2 garlic cloves, minced
- ½ teaspoon Garam masala
- ½ teaspoon ground chili
- 1 teaspoon ground coriander
- 1 teaspoon ground cumin
- 1 teaspoon ground ginger
- 2 tomatoes, diced
- 1 tablespoon fresh coriander
- Salt as needed

Directions

1. Make the marinade by mixing coconut cream and Garam Masala together
2. Rub it all over the lamb and allow it to chill for 24 hours

3. Set your pot to Sauté mode and add oil, whole spices and sizzle them briefly until aroma is released
4. Add garlic and stir well
5. Add the rest of the powdered spices and cook for a while, add fresh tomatoes, water and tomato puree
6. Add the marinated lamb and give it a nice stir
7. Cancel the Sauté mode and lock up the lid
8. Cook on HIGH pressure for 10 minutes
9. Do a quick release
10. Remove the lid and set the pot to Sauté mode
11. Stir well for a few minutes and check the seasoning
12. Serve over some cauliflower rice and enjoy!

Nutrition Values (Per Serving)

- Calories: 563
- Fat: 22g
- Carbohydrates: 41g
- Protein: 49g

Chapter 7: Poultry Recipes

Simple Pineapple Chicken

Serving: 4

Prep Time: 5 minutes

Cook Time: 30-35 minutes

Ingredients

- 2 pounds chicken breasts, boneless and skinless
- 2 cups pineapple chunks, divided
- ½ sweet onion, diced
- 2 garlic cloves, minced
- ½ teaspoon cumin
- 1 teaspoon paprika
- 2 teaspoons chili powder
- Salt to taste
- ½ cup pineapple juice
- 1 chipotle chili pepper, in adobo sauce, chopped
- 1 poblano pepper, sliced
- ¼ cup fresh cilantro, chopped
- 1 teaspoon lime juice

Directions

1. Add chicken t your Instant Pot
2. Add 1 cup pineapple and remaining ingredients to your pot (Except cilantro and lime juice)
3. Lock lid and cook on HIGH pressure for 25 minutes
4. Release pressure naturally over 10 minutes
5. Take chicken out and shred using forks
6. Make the salsa by mixing pineapple chunks, cilantro, and lime juice
7. Season and serve

8. Enjoy!

Nutrition Values (Per Serving)

- Calories: 508
- Fat: 17g
- Carbohydrates: 18g
- Protein: 67g

Feisty Turmeric Chicken

Serving: 4

Prep Time: 5 minutes

Cook Time: 20-26 minutes

Ingredients

- 3 tablespoons ghee
- 1 onion, chopped
- 3 garlic cloves, minced
- 1 teaspoon ginger, minced
- 2 pounds chicken thighs, boneless and skinless
- Salt and pepper to taste
- 1 and ½ tablespoons turmeric
- 1 tablespoon Garam masala
- 1 tablespoon cumin
- 1 cinnamon stick
- 2 tablespoons lemon juice
- 1 teaspoon apple cider vinegar
- 1 cup chicken broth
- 1 cup of coconut milk

Directions

1. Set your Instant Pot to Sauté mode and add ghee, let the ghee heat up
2. Add onion, garlic, and ginger
3. Mix in bay leaves and cook for 6 minutes
4. Add chicken, salt, pepper, spices and stir in remaining ingredients
5. Mix well
6. Simmer for 5 minutes
7. Lock lid and cook on POULTRY mode for 20 minutes
8. Release pressure naturally over 10 minutes
9. Serve with a sprinkle of chopped almond if desired

10. Enjoy!

<u>Nutrition Values (Per Serving)</u>

- Calories: 556
- Fat: 33g
- Carbohydrates: 7g
- Protein: 55g

Sweet Potato and Chicken Curry

Serving: 4

Prep Time: 5 minutes

Cook Time: 25 minutes

Ingredients

- 2 teaspoons ghee
- 1 onion, diced
- 3 garlic cloves, minced
- 1-pound chicken breast, cubed
- 1 sweet potato, cubed
- 2 cups green beans, trimmed and sliced
- 1 red pepper, sliced
- 3 tablespoons curry powder
- ½ cup chicken broth
- 1 teaspoon ground turmeric
- 1 teaspoon cumin
- ½ teaspoon cayenne
- Salt to taste
- 2 cups of coconut milk

Directions

1. Set your Instant Pot to Sauté mode and add ghee, add onion and garlic, cook for 3 minutes
2. Add chicken and remaining ingredients to your Instant Pot
3. Lock lid and cook on HIGH pressure for 12 minutes
4. Naturally, release pressure over 10 minutes
5. Stir in coconut milk
6. Serve and enjoy!

Nutrition Values (Per Serving)

- Calories: 412
- Fat: 27g
- Carbohydrates: 20g
- Protein: 24g

Delightful Harissa Chicken

Serving: 4

Prep Time: 5 minutes

Cook Time: 10 minutes

Ingredients

- 2 chipotle peppers, in adobo sauce
- 2 teaspoons adobo sauce
- 1 teaspoon lemon juice
- 2 red peppers
- 1 tablespoon apple cider vinegar
- 1 teaspoon ground cumin
- 1 teaspoon ground coriander
- ½ teaspoon caraway seeds
- 4 garlic cloves, minced
- Salt and pepper to taste
- 1 tablespoon avocado oil
- ½ cup onion, diced
- 1 and ½ pounds of chicken breast

Directions

1. Add listed ingredients (except oil, onion, breast) to a food processor, process until smooth
2. Set your pot to Sauté mode and add onion, cook for 3 minutes
3. Add chicken and add pureed sauce on top
4. Lock lid and cook on HIGH pressure for 7 minutes
5. Quick release pressure
6. Shred chicken and drizzle cooking liquid on top
7. Serve and enjoy!

Nutrition Values (Per Serving)

- Calories: 225
- Fat: 5g
- Carbohydrates: 5g
- Protein: 37g

Genius Lime Chicken

Serving: 4

Prep Time: 5 minutes

Cook Time: 6 minutes

Ingredients

- 2 pounds chicken breast, skinless and boneless
- ½ teaspoon liquid smoke
- 5 garlic cloves, minced
- 1 teaspoon onion powder
- 1 teaspoon cumin
- 1 and ½ teaspoon chili powder
- 2 fresh limes juice
- ¼ teaspoon black pepper
- 1 teaspoon salt

Directions

1. Add chicken to your Instant Pot
2. Add lemon juice, sprinkle seasoning s over chicken
3. Add garlic and liquid smoke
4. Rub all over and lock lid, cook on HIGH pressure for 6 minutes
5. Release pressure naturally over 10 minutes
6. Shred chicken and season with salt and pepper
7. Serve and enjoy!

Nutrition Values (Per Serving)

- Calories: 444
- Fat: 17g
- Carbohydrates: 2g
- Protein: 66g

Creative Lemon Garlic Chicken

Serving: 6

Prep Time: 5 minutes

Cook Time: 15 minutes

Ingredients

- 2 pounds chicken thigh, boneless
- ½ cup chicken stock
- 1-pound green beans
- 1-pound potatoes
- 1 teaspoon herbs de Provence
- 1 lemon, juiced
- 5 garlic cloves, crushed
- 3 tablespoons extra virgin olive oil
- 4 tablespoons ghee
- ¼ teaspoon black pepper
- ½ teaspoon salt

Directions

1. Add ghee to your Instant Pot and set it to Sauté mode, add garlic, lemon juice, pepper, salt and stir
2. Add chicken and Sauté for 3-4 minutes
3. Add remaining ingredients and stir
4. Lock lid and cook on HIGH pressure for 15 minutes
5. Naturally, release pressure over 10 minutes
6. Stir and serve

Nutrition Values (Per Serving)

- Calories: 504
- Fat: 27g
- Carbohydrates: 18g
- Protein: 46g

The Authentic Chicken Tikka Masala

Serving: 4

Prep Time: 5 minutes

Cook Time: 4 hours 5 minutes

Ingredients

- 1 onion, chopped
- 3 garlic cloves, minced
- 1 ginger, chopped
- 1 cup tomatoes, chopped
- 2 teaspoons paprika
- 1 teaspoon ground turmeric
- 1 teaspoon garam masala
- 1 teaspoon ground coriander
- 2 teaspoons cumin
- ½ cup chicken broth
- 1 and ½ pounds chicken breast, boneless and skinless
- ½ cup of coconut milk
- 1 teaspoon lemon juice

Directions

1. Take a bowl and mix in onion, garlic, ginger, tomatoes, and mix
2. Stir in spices
3. Add mixture to your Instant Pot, place chicken on top
4. Add broth and lock lid, cook on SLOW COOKER mode for 4 hours
5. Stir in coconut milk and lemon

Nutrition Values (Per Serving)

- Calories: 301
- Fat: 21g
- Carbohydrates: 8g
- Protein: 38g

Pressure Cooked Crab Legs

Serving: 4

Prep Time: 10 minutes

Cook Time: 7 minutes

Ingredients

- 2 pounds crab legs
- 1 cup of water
- 1 cup white wine vinegar
- ½ cup clarified butter
- 1 lemon, sliced into wedges

Directions

1. Add water to Instant Pot, add wine vinegar
2. Add crab legs
3. Lock lid and cook on HIGH pressure for 7 minutes
4. Release pressure naturally over 10 minutes
5. Open and add melted butter with a dash of lemon
6. Serve and enjoy!

Nutrition Values (Per Serving)

- Calories: 191
- Fat: 1g
- Carbohydrates: 0g
- Protein: 41g

Everyday Chicken Wings

Serving: 4

Prep Time: 5 minutes

Cook Time: 6 minutes

Ingredients

- 1- and 1/3-pounds chicken wings
- 1 and ½ teaspoon smoked salt
- 4 tablespoons taco seasoning

Directions

1. Take a dish and make in taco seasoning, smoked salt
2. Coat all chicken wings with seasoning mixture
3. Add 1 cup water into pot and place trivet
4. Place seasoned wings over the trivet
5. Lock lid and cook on HIGH pressure for 10 minutes
6. Release pressure naturally over 10 minutes
7. Transfer wings to baking sheet and broil for 10 minutes
8. Serve and enjoy!

Nutrition Values (Per Serving)

- Calories: 207
- Fat: 7g
- Carbohydrates: 3g
- Protein: 29g

Chapter 8: Seafood Recipes

Juicy Salmon and Orange

Serving: 4

Prep Time: 10 minutes

Cook Time: 15 minutes

Ingredients

- 4 salmon fillets
- 1 cup of orange juice
- 2 tablespoons cornstarch juice
- 1 teaspoon orange peel, grated
- 1 teaspoon black pepper

Directions

1. Add all of the listed ingredients to your pot
2. Lock up the lid and cook on HIGH pressure for 12 minutes
3. Release the pressure naturally
4. Open and serve!

Nutrition Values (Per Serving)

- Calories: 582
- Fat: 20g
- Carbohydrates: 7g
- Protein: 33g

Hearty Salmon Patties

Serving: 4

Prep Time: 10 minutes

Cook Time: 5-10 minutes

Ingredients

- 2 salmon fillets
- ¼ cup onion, chopped
- 2 stalks green onion, chopped
- 1 whole egg
- Almond meal as needed
- Salt and pepper to taste
- 2 tablespoons olive oil

Direction

1. Add a cup of water to your pot and place a steamer rack on top
2. Place the fish
3. Season the fish with salt and pepper and lock up the lid
4. Cook on HIGH pressure for 3 minutes
5. Quick release the pressure
6. Remove the fish and allow it to cool
7. Break the fillets into a bowl and add egg, yellow and green onions
8. Add ½ a cup of almond meal and mix with your hand
9. Divide the mixture into patties
10. Take a large skillet and place it over medium heat
11. Add oil and cook the patties until slightly browned

Nutrition Values (Per Serving)

- Calories: 238
- Fat: 15g
- Carbohydrates: 2g
- Protein: 23g

Juicy Coconut Fish Curry

Serving: 4

Prep Time: 10 minutes

Cook Time: 5 minutes

Ingredients

- 1 (14 ounces) can coconut milk
- Juice of 1 lime
- 1 tablespoon red curry paste
- 1 teaspoon fish sauce
- 1 teaspoon date paste
- 2 teaspoons Sriracha
- 2 garlic cloves, minced
- 1 teaspoon ground turmeric
- 1 teaspoon ground ginger
- ½ teaspoon salt
- ½ teaspoon white pepper
- 1-pound sea bass/cod cut into 1-inch cube
- 3 lime wedges

Direction

1. Take a large sized bowl and add coconut milk, lime juice, red curry paste, fish sauce, date paste, coconut amino, garlic sriracha, ginger, turmeric, white pepper, sea salt
2. Mix well
3. Place the sea bass/cod in the bottom of your Instant Pot
4. Pour coconut milk mixture over the fish and lock up the lid
5. Cook for 3 minutes, do a quick release
6. Transfer the fish and broth into three individual bowls and garnish them with chopped up cilantro
7. Serve and enjoy!

Nutrition Values (Per Serving)

- Calories: 276
- Fat: 21g
- Carbohydrates: 4g
- Protein: 18g

Authentic Sock Eye Salmon

Serving: 4

Prep Time: 10 minutes

Cook Time: 10 minutes

Ingredients

- 3-4 ounces Alaskan Sockeye Salmon Fillets
- 1 cup of water
- 2 cups lemon, sliced
- Salt and pepper to taste

Direction

1. Add the steamer basket to your pot
2. Add 1 cup of water
3. Lay the fish on your steamer rack
4. Season with salt and pepper
5. Place lime slices on top
6. Lock up the lid and steam for 5 minutes
7. Quick release the pressure and serve over vegetables
8. Enjoy!

Nutrition Values (Per Serving)

- Calories: 487
- Fat: 20g
- Carbohydrates: 0g
- Protein: 77g

Alternative Fancy Cod Dish

Serving: 4

Prep Time: 10 minutes

Cook Time: 15 minutes

Ingredients

- 6 fresh/frozen cod fillets
- 3 tablespoons clarified butter
- 1 lemon, juiced
- 1 onion, sliced
- 1 teaspoon salt
- ½ teaspoon pepper
- 1 teaspoon oregano
- 1 can (28 ounces) tomatoes, diced

Direction

1. Set your pot to Sauté mode and add the clarified butter
2. Once the butter is hot, add the remaining ingredients and give it a nice stir
3. Sauté for 10 minutes
4. Arrange the fish portions in the sauce and use your spoon to cover the pieces with the sauce
5. Lock up the lid and cook on HIGH pressure for 5 minutes
6. Do a quick release and serve with the sauce
7. Enjoy!

Nutrition Values (Per Serving)

- Calories: 301
- Fat: 14g
- Carbohydrates: 5g
- Protein: 47g

Cool Salmon and Broccoli

Serving: 4

Prep Time: 10 minutes

Cook Time: 4 minutes

Ingredients

- 2 and ½ pounds salmon fillets
- 2 and ½ ounces broccoli
- 9 ounces new potatoes
- 1 teaspoon butter
- Salt and pepper to taste
- Fresh Italian herbs for garnish

Directions

1. Chop the broccoli into florets and keep them on the side
2. ½ a cup of water to your Instant Pot
3. Season the potatoes with salt, fresh herbs, and pepper
4. Season the salmon and broccoli with salt and pepper
5. Add potatoes to a steaming rack and smother them with butter
6. Transfer to your Instant Pot
7. Lock up the lid and cook for 2 minutes on the Steam setting
8. Quick release the pressure
9. Add broccoli florets and salmon and steam cook for 2 minutes more
10. Quick release
11. Serve and enjoy!

Nutrition Values (Per Serving)

- Calories: 556
- Fat: 40g
- Carbohydrates: 11g
- Protein: 39g

Pineapple and Shrimp Delight

Serving: 4

Prep Time: 10 minutes

Cook Time: 5 minutes

Ingredients

- 1 large red bell pepper, cleaned and sliced
- ½ cup unsweetened pineapple juice
- ¼ cup dry white wine vinegar
- 2 tablespoons coconut amino
- 2 tablespoons Thai sweet chili sauce
- 1-pound large shrimp
- 1 tablespoon ground chili paste
- 4 scallions, chopped
- 1 and ½ cups unsweetened pineapple chunks

Directions

1. Drain the juice from pineapple and set the pineapple chunks on the side
2. Measure out ½ a cup of pineapple juice
3. Add red bell pepper, pineapple juice, rice, wine, chili sauce, soy sauce, chili paste, and chopped scallions to the Instant Pot
4. Place the shrimp on top
5. Lock up the lid and cook on HIGH pressure for 2 minutes
6. Naturally, release the pressure over 10 minutes
7. Add pineapple chunks and scallion greens
8. Mix well and serve!

Nutrition Values (Per Serving)

- Calories: 299
- Fat: 5g
- Carbohydrates: 54g
- Protein: 8g

Hearty Cooked Lobster

Serving: 4

Prep Time: 10 minutes

Cook Time: 7 minutes

Ingredients

- 2 lobsters
- 1 cup of water
- 1 cup white wine vinegar
- 1 cup clarified butter

Directions

1. Add the listed ingredients to your Instant Pot
2. Lock up the lid and cook on HIGH pressure for 7 minutes
3. Release the pressure naturally
4. Open and add some extra melted butter
5. Serve and enjoy!

Nutrition Values (Per Serving)

- Calories: 230
- Fat: 16g
- Carbohydrates: 4g
- Protein: 17g

Chapter 9: Vegetarian Recipes

Gentle Cauliflower Soup

Serving: 6

Prep Time: 5 minutes

Cook Time: 25-30 minutes

Ingredients

- 1 small cauliflower head, chopped
- 4 cups chicken broth
- 14 ounces can coconut milk
- 1 teaspoon turmeric
- 2 tablespoons curry powder
- 1 teaspoon ginger, grated
- 2 teaspoons garlic, minced
- 1 large sweet potato, peeled and diced
- 1 cup onion, diced
- 1 cup carrots, diced
- 1 tablespoon extra-virgin olive oil

Directions

1. Add oil to your Instant Pot and set it to Sauté mode
2. Add onion, carrots and Sauté for 3 minutes
3. Add turmeric, curry powder, ginger, garlic, cauliflower, sweet potato, and stir
4. Add broth, coconut milk, stir
5. Lock lid and cook on SOUP mode using default settings
6. Quick release pressure
7. Use an immersion blender to puree the soup
8. Season and enjoy!

Nutrition Values (Per Serving)

- Calories: 240
- Fat: 17g
- Carbohydrates: 16g
- Protein: 6g

Amazing Butter and Garlic Potatoes

Serving: 4

Prep Time: 10 minutes

Cook Time: 4-6 minutes

Ingredients

- 1-pound new potatoes
- 3 teaspoons garlic puree
- 3 tablespoons coconut butter
- ¼ cup fresh herbs, chopped
- Salt and pepper to taste

Directions

1. Add 1 cup water to your Instant Pot, place a steamer rack in pot
2. Add listed ingredients to steamer rack, stir well to ensure that the potato is coated evenly with butter, garlic puree, and herbs
3. and lock lid, cook on HIGH pressure for 4 minutes
4. Quick release pressure
5. Serve warm and enjoy!

Nutrition Values (Per Serving)

- Calories: 319
- Fat: 15g
- Carbohydrates: 43g
- Protein: 5g

Healthy Brussels and Pine Nuts

Serving: 6

Prep Time: 5 minutes

Cook Time: 3-5 minutes

Ingredients

- 1-pound Brussels sprouts, washed and cut
- 1 cup pomegranate seeds
- ¼ cup pine nuts, toasted
- Salt and pepper to taste

Directions

1. Add 1 cup water to your Instant Pot
2. Place steamer basket inside the pot
3. Add Brussels to the steamer basket and lock lid, cook on HIGH pressure for 3 minutes
4. Quick release pressure
5. Transfer sprouts to dish and season with salt and pepper
6. Sprinkle pomegranate seeds and pine nuts
7. Serve and enjoy!

Nutrition Values (Per Serving)

- Calories: 124
- Fat: 6g
- Carbohydrates: 11g
- Protein: 5g

Ghee Dredged Baby Carrots

Serving: 6

Prep Time: 5 minutes

Cook Time: 2-5 minutes

Ingredients

- 1-pound baby carrots
- 1 cup of water
- 1 tablespoon clarified ghee
- 1 tablespoon fresh mint leaves, chopped
- Salt as needed

Directions

1. Place a steamer rack on top of your pot and add the carrots
2. Add water
3. Lock up the lid and cook at HIGH pressure for 2 minutes
4. Do a quick release
5. Pass the carrots through a strainer and drain them
6. Wipe the insert clean
7. Return the insert to the pot and set the pot to Sauté mode
8. Add clarified butter and allow it to melt
9. Add mint and Sauté for 30 seconds
10. Add carrots to the insert and Sauté well
11. Remove them and sprinkle with a bit of salt on top
12. Enjoy!

Nutrition Values (Per Serving)

- Calories: 131
- Fat: 10g
- Carbohydrates: 11g
- Protein: 1g

Easy Steamed Artichokes

Serving: 6

Prep Time: 5 minutes

Cook Time: 10 minutes

Ingredients

- 2 medium artichokes
- 1 lemon, sliced in half
- 2 tablespoons homemade Whole30 Mayo (recipe included)
- 1 teaspoon Dijon mustard
- 1 pinch paprika

Directions

1. Wash the artichokes carefully and remove any damaged outer leaves
2. Trim the spines and cut off the upper edge
3. Wipe the cut edges using a lemon half
4. Slice the stem (if present) and peel the stem and chop it up. Keep it for later use
5. Add a cup of water to the pot and place the steamer basket on top
6. Transfer the chokes to the steamer basket a squeeze a bit of lemon on top
7. Lock up the lid and cook on HIGH pressure for 10 minutes
8. Allow the pressure to release naturally and enjoy!

Nutrition Values (Per Serving)

- Calories: 77
- Fat: 5g
- Carbohydrates: 0g
- Protein: 2g

Butter and Garlic Green Beans

Serving: 6

Prep Time: 5 minutes

Cook Time: 3-5 minutes

Ingredients

- 1-pound fresh green beans
- 1 and ¼ cups of water
- 1 garlic clove, minced
- 2 tablespoons clarified butter
- Salt and pepper to taste

Directions

1. Add listed ingredients to your Instant Pot, gently stir
2. Lock lid and cook on LOW pressure for 5 minutes
3. Quick release pressure
4. Open the lid and serve, enjoy!

Nutrition Values (Per Serving)

- Calories: 87
- Fat: 5g
- Carbohydrates: 8g
- Protein: 2g

Mashed Cauliflower Meal

Serving: 6

Prep Time: 5 minutes

Cook Time: 3-5 minutes

Ingredients

- 1 large cauliflower head, cut into florets
- 1 cup of water
- 1 tablespoon clarified butter
- 1/8 teaspoon salt
- 1/8 teaspoon pepper
- ¼ teaspoon garlic powder
- 1 handful chives

Directions

1. Core your cauliflower carefully into large-sized chunks
2. Add your steamer basket on top of your Instant Pot and add the cauliflowers to the pot
3. Add water to the pot
4. Lock up the lid and allow it to cook for about 3-5 minutes over high pressure
5. Quickly release the pot
6. Remove the inner pot and drain the water
7. Return the cauliflower to the inner pot
8. Add butter and seasoning
9. Puree everything with an immersion blender
10. Stir and serve!

Nutrition Values (Per Serving)

- Calories: 739
- Fat: 56g
- Carbohydrates: 55g
- Protein: 8g

Healthy Potato Gratin

Serving: 6

Prep Time: 5 minutes

Cook Time: 5 minutes

Ingredients

- 3 tablespoons olive oil
- 3 cups parsnips, sliced
- 3 garlic cloves, chopped
- 2 cups vegetable broth
- 1 tablespoon pepper
- 1 tablespoon garlic powder
- 1 cup Whole30 friendly Mayo

Directions

1. Set your pot to Sauté mode and add ingredients except for mayo
2. Lock up the lid and cook on HIGH pressure for 5 minutes
3. Release the pressure naturally
4. Open the lid and spread a bit of Whole30 mayo all over
5. Set your pot to Sauté mode and warm for a while
6. Enjoy!

Nutrition Values (Per Serving)

- Calories: 201
- Fat: 10g
- Carbohydrates: 22g
- Protein: 6g

Mixed Summer Vegetable Platter

Serving: 6

Prep Time: 5 minutes

Cook Time: 20 minutes

Ingredients

- 1-pound raw almonds
- 1 bay leaf
- 2 medium tomatoes, chopped
- ½ cup green pepper, chopped
- ½ cup sweet onion, diced
- ¼ cup hot pepper, diced
- ¼ cup celery, diced
- 2 tablespoons olive oil
- ¾ teaspoon salt
- ¼ teaspoon fresh ground black pepper

Directions

1. Add 2 cups water to your Instant Pot alongside bay leaves and almonds and other vegetables
2. Lock lid and cook for 20 minutes at HIGH pressure
3. Quick release pressure
4. Take a bowl and add almonds and diced vegetables, take another small bowl and mix in oil, lemon juice, pepper, salt
5. Pour dressing over salad and toss

Nutrition Values (Per Serving)

- Calories: 140
- Fat: 4g
- Carbohydrates: 24g
- Protein: 5g

Tasty Carrot and Kale Bowl

Serving: 6

Prep Time: 5 minutes

Cook Time: 5 minutes

Ingredients

- 10 ounces kale, chopped
- 1 tablespoon ghee
- 1 medium onion, sliced
- 3 medium carrots, cut into half inch pieces
- 5 garlic cloves, peeled and chopped
- ½ cup chicken broth
- Salt and pepper to taste
- Vinegar as needed
- ½ teaspoon red pepper flakes

Directions

1. Set your pot to Sauté mode and add ghee, allow it to melt
2. Add chopped up onion and carrot and Sauté until tender
3. Add garlic and keep cooking until a nice fragrance comes
4. Add kale and pour chicken broth
5. Sprinkle salt and pepper
6. Lock up the lid and cook for 8 minutes at HIGH pressure
7. Release the pressure naturally
8. Open up the lid and give a swirl to make sure that everything is in order. Pour down the vinegar and sprinkle some more pepper flakes if spicy is what you prefer.

Nutrition Values (Per Serving)

- Calories: 41.1
- Fat: 2.1g
- Carbohydrates: 5.5g
- Protein: 1.4g

Indian Spinach and Mustard Dish

Serving: 4

Prep Time: 10 minutes

Cook Time: 15-20 minutes

Ingredients

- 1-pound spinach, rinsed
- 1-pound mustard leaves, rinsed
- 2 tablespoons ghee
- 2 medium onion, diced
- 2-inch knob ginger, minced
- 4 garlic cloves, minced
- 2 teaspoons salt
- 1 teaspoons coriander
- 1 teaspoon cumin
- 1 teaspoon Garam Masala
- ½ teaspoon turmeric
- ½ teaspoon pepper
- Pinch of kasoori methi

Directions

1. Set your pot to Sauté mode and allow the ghee to melt
2. Once ghee has melted, add ginger onion and spices and give it a nice stir and fry for 2-3 minutes
3. Lock up the lid and cook for 15 minutes on poultry setting
4. Once the cooking is done, allow the pressure to release naturally over 10 minutes
5. Add the pot contents to a blender and blend well
6. Alternatively, you may use an immersion blender to blend them well until you have reached your desired consistency
7. Serve with a topping of ghee and enjoy!

Nutrition Values (Per Serving)

- Calories: 205
- Fat: 12g
- Carbohydrates: 14g
- Protein: 14g

The All-Natural Sugar-Free Applesauce

Serving: 4

Prep Time: 10 minutes

Cook Time: 10 minutes

Ingredients

- 12 medium apples, diced and peeled
- Scant ½ cup of water

Directions

1. Transfer the peeled and diced apples to your pot
2. Add water
3. Take a parchment paper and cut it into a large circle (big enough to cover the apples inside the pot)
4. Place the paper on top of the apples
5. Lock up the lid and cook on HIGH pressure for 10 minutes
6. Release the pressure naturally and open the lid, discard the paper
7. Use an immersion blender to blend the whole mix until smooth
8. Enjoy!

Nutrition Values (Per Serving)

- Calories: 166
- Fats: 0.4g
- Carbs:15g
- Fiber:3g

Rhubarb and Strawberry Compote

Serving: 4

Prep Time: 10 minutes

Cook Time: 20 minutes

Ingredients

- 2 pounds rhubarb
- ½ cup of water
- 1-pound strawberries
- 3 tablespoons date paste
- Fresh mint to taste

Directions

1. Peel the rhubarb using a paring knife and chop it up ½ inch pieces
2. Add the chopped-up rhubarb to your pot alongside water
3. Lock up the lid and cook on HIGH pressure for 10 minutes
4. Stem and quarter your strawberries and keep them on the side
5. Add the strawberries and date paste, give it a nice stir
6. Lock up the lid and cook on HIGH pressure for 20 minutes
7. Release the pressure naturally and enjoy the compote!

Nutrition Values (Per Serving)

- Calories: 41.1
- Fat: 2.1g
- Carbohydrates: 5.5g
- Protein: 1.4g

Chapter 10: Soup and Stew Recipes

Exquisite Lobster Bisque

Serving: 4

Prep Time: 10 minutes

Cook Time: 6 minutes

Ingredients

- 1 cup carrots, diced
- 1 cup celery, diced
- 29 ounces tomatoes, diced
- 1 garlic clove, minced
- 1 tablespoon butter
- 32-ounce low sodium chicken broth
- 1 teaspoon dill
- ½ teaspoon paprika
- 4 lobster tail
- 1-pint heavy whip cream +

Directions

1. Add butter, garlic, and minced shallots to a microwave safe bowl
2. Microwave for 2-3 minutes on HIGH
3. Add tomatoes, celery, carrot, minced shallots, garlic to your Instant Pot
4. Add chicken broth and spices to the Pot
5. Use a knife to cut the lobster tails if you prefer and add them to the Instant Pot
6. Lock up the lid and cook on HIGH pressure for 4 minutes
7. Release the pressure naturally over 10 minutes
8. Use an immersion blender to puree to your desired chunkiness
9. Serve and enjoy!

Nutrition Values (Per Serving)

- Calories: 437
- Fat: 17g
- Carbohydrates: 21g
- Protein: 38g

Simple Lamb Stew

Serving: 6

Prep Time: 5 minutes

Cook Time: 25 minutes

Ingredients

- 2 pounds lamb stew meat, cut into 1-inch cubes
- 1 acorn squash
- 3 large carrots, sliced
- 1 large yellow onion
- 1 bay leaf
- 6 garlic cloves, sliced
- 3 tablespoons broth
- ¼-1/2 teaspoon salt

Directions

1. Peel the squash and deseed them
2. Cube the squash
3. Slice up the carrots into circles
4. Peel the onion in half and slice the halves into half moons
5. Add all of the ingredients (including veggies) to your pot and lock up the lid
6. Cook on HIGH pressure for 25 minutes
7. Release the pressure naturally and serve!

Nutrition Values (Per Serving)

- Calories: 271
- Fat: 20g
- Carbohydrates: 5g
- Protein: 13g

Slightly "Eastern" Lamb Stew

Serving: 6

Prep Time: 5 minutes

Cook Time: 25 minutes

Ingredients

- 2 tablespoons ghee
- 1 and ½ pounds lamb stew meat, cut into 1 and ½ inch cubes
- 1 onion, diced
- 5-6 garlic clove, chopped
- 1 teaspoon salt
- 1 teaspoon pepper
- 1 teaspoon cumin
- 1 teaspoon coriander
- 1 teaspoon turmeric
- 1 teaspoon cinnamon
- 1 teaspoon cumin seeds
- ½ teaspoon chili flakes
- 2 tablespoons tomato paste
- ¼ cup apple cider vinegar
- 1 and ¼ cup chicken stock
- ¼ cup dried apricots, chopped
- 2 tablespoons date paste

Directions

1. Set your pot to Sauté mode and add ghee, allow it to heat up
2. Add onion and Sauté for 3-4 minutes until a nice fragrance comes
3. Add lamb, salt, garlic, and spices and Sauté them for 5 minutes until they release a nice fragrance
4. Add vinegar, date paste, tomato paste, stock and apricots and stir well
5. Lock up the lid and cook on HIGH pressure for 60 minutes

6. Release the pressure naturally
7. Serve with a garnish of fresh cilantro
8. Enjoy!

Nutrition Values (Per Serving)

- Calories: 563
- Fat: 22g
- Carbohydrates: 41g
- Protein: 49g

The Original Enchilada Soup

Serving: 6

Prep Time: 5 minutes

Cook Time: 15 minutes

Ingredients

- 1 and ½ pounds chicken thigh, skinless and boneless
- ½ teaspoon ground pepper
- ½ teaspoon smoked paprika
- 1 teaspoon oregano
- 1 tablespoon chili powder
- 1 tablespoon cumin
- ½ cup of water
- 2 cups chicken broth
- 3 garlic cloves, minced
- 1 onion, sliced
- 1 bell pepper, sliced
- 14 ounces can, tomatoes, crushed
- ½ teaspoon salt

Directions

1. Add listed ingredients to your Instant Pot and stir
2. Lock lid and cook on HIGH pressure for 20 minutes
3. Release pressure naturally over 10 minutes
4. Shred chicken using a fork
5. Stir and serve
6. Enjoy!

Nutrition Values (Per Serving)

- Calories: 268
- Fat: 9g

- Carbohydrates: 8g
- Protein: 35g

Very Yummy Chicken Soup

Serving: 4

Prep Time: 5 minutes

Cook Time: 25-30 minutes

Ingredients

- 1 and ½ pounds chicken drumsticks
- 4 cups chicken broth
- 2 bay leaves
- 1 small onion, diced
- 1 rutabaga, peeled and diced
- 1 parsnip, peeled and diced
- 2 medium carrots, peeled and diced
- 2 celery ribs, sliced
- ½ teaspoon black pepper

Directions

1. Add listed ingredients to Instant Pot and gently stir
2. Lock lid and cook on SOUP mode on default settings
3. Release pressure naturally over 10 minutes
4. Remove meat from pot and shred, discard bones
5. Return meat to pot and season with salt and pepper
6. Serve and enjoy!

Nutrition Values (Per Serving)

- Calories: 411
- Fat: 11g
- Carbohydrates: 20g
- Protein: 3g

Wow-Worthy Creamy Onion Soup

Serving: 6

Prep Time: 5 minutes

Cook Time: 15 minutes

Ingredients

- 8 cups yellow onion, sliced
- 2 fresh thyme sprigs
- 2 bay leaves
- 6 cups vegetable stock
- 1 tablespoon balsamic vinegar
- 1 tablespoon balsamic vinegar
- 2 tablespoons coconut oil
- 1 teaspoon salt

Directions

1. Add oil to your Instant Pot and set your pot to Sauté mode
2. Add onion to the pot and Sauté for 15 minutes
3. Add thyme, bay leaves, salt, stock, vinegar, and stir
4. Lock lid and cook on HIGH pressure for 10 minutes
5. Release pressure naturally over 10 minutes
6. Discard thyme and bay leaves, use an immersion blender to puree the soup until smooth
7. Stir and enjoy!

Nutrition Values (Per Serving)

- Calories: 111
- Fat: 7g
- Carbohydrates: 16g
- Protein: 55g

Hearty Asparagus Soup

Serving: 6

Prep Time: 5 minutes

Cook Time: 45-50 minutes

Ingredients

- 2 pounds organic chicken thigh
- 1 cup fresh pineapple chunks
- ½ cup coconut cream
- 1 teaspoon cinnamon
- 1/8 teaspoon salt
- 2 tablespoons coconut amino
- ½ cup green onion, chopped

Directions

1. Set your pot to Sauté mode and add ghee
2. Allow the ghee to melt and add diced up onion, cook for about 5 minutes until the onions are caramelized
3. Add pressed garlic, ham, broth and simmer for 2-3 minutes
4. Add thyme and asparagus and lock up the lid
5. Cook on SOUP mode for 45 minutes
6. Release the pressure naturally and enjoy!

Nutrition Values (Per Serving)

- Calories: 161
- Fat: 8g
- Carbohydrates: 16g
- Protein: 6g

Nice Apple Cabbage and Beet Stew

Serving: 6

Prep Time: 5 minutes

Cook Time: 3-5 minutes

Ingredients

- ½ cabbage head, chopped
- 2 beets, chopped
- 1 apple, diced
- 2 tablespoons parsley
- 1 tablespoon fresh ginger, grated
- 2 small carrots, chopped
- 1 small onion, chopped
- 4 cups chicken broth
- Salt and pepper to taste

Directions

1. Add listed ingredients to Instant Pot
2. Gently stir
3. Lock lid and cook on HIGH pressure for 20 minutes
4. Quick release pressure
5. Stir well and enjoy!

Nutrition Values (Per Serving)

- Calories: 134
- Fat: 2g
- Carbohydrates: 23g
- Protein: 5g

Cabbage and Carrot "Hearty Celery" Soup

Serving: 6

Prep Time: 5 minutes

Cook Time: 3-5 minutes

Ingredients

- 1 small cabbage head, chopped
- 3 cups chicken broth
- 1 tablespoon lemon juice
- 3 tablespoons apple cider vinegar
- 3 garlic cloves, minced
- 28 ounces tomatoes, chopped
- 3 celery stalks, chopped
- 3 carrots, chopped
- 1 onion, chopped

Directions

1. Add listed ingredients to Instant Pot, stir
2. Lock lid and cook on HIGH pressure for 15 minutes
3. Quick release pressure
4. Stir well and serve
5. Enjoy!
6. Alternatively, you may use an immersion blender to smoothen the soup and serve as well!

Nutrition Values (Per Serving)

- Calories: 148
- Fat: 2g
- Carbohydrates: 27g
- Protein: 8g

Friendly Butternut Squash Soup

Serving: 4

Prep Time: 10 minutes

Cook Time: 30 minutes

Ingredients

- 1 teaspoon extra virgin olive oil
- 1 large onion, chopped
- 2 garlic cloves, minced
- 1 tablespoon curry powder
- 3 pounds butternut squash, cut into 1-inch cubes, peeled
- 3 cups of water
- ½ cup of coconut milk
- Hulled pumpkin seeds and dried cranberries for topping

Directions

1. Set your pot to Sauté mode and add olive oil, allow the oil to heat up
2. Add onions and Sauté for about 8 minutes
3. Add garlic and curry powder and Sauté for 1 minute more
4. Remove the powder and add butternut squash, salt, and water
5. Lock up the lid and cook on HIGH pressure for 30 minutes
6. Release the pressure naturally over 10 minutes
7. Open the lid and blend everything into a puree using an immersion blender
8. Stir in coconut milk and season with some salt
9. Serve with a topping of dried cranberries, enjoy!

Nutrition Values (Per Serving)

- Calories: 124
- Fat: 6g
- Carbohydrates: 18g
- Protein: 2g

Conclusion

I wholeheartedly thank you for purchasing and downloading my book. I am delighted that you found the book and the recipes interesting enough to read it through to the end.

The next step for you is to start trying out these recipes and experiment with them until you find your next big winning dish.

If you are happy with the contents, then I would kindly ask you to leave an honest review on Amazon. Being an aspiring writer, your true words would help me and my book a lot and encourage me to trim down my flaws and write more helpful books in the future.

Your kind gesture would be immensely appreciated by me.

Be safe and stay healthy!

60594569R00059

Made in the USA
Columbia, SC
15 June 2019